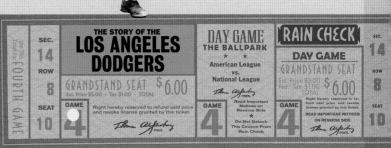

DISCARDED

Published by Creative Education
P.O. Box 227, Mankato, Minnesota 56002
Creative Education is an imprint of The Creative Company

Design and production by Blue Design
Printed in the United States of America

Photographs by Corbis (Bettmann), Getty Images (Andrew D. Bernstein, Bernstein Associates, Lisa Blumenfeld, Diamond Images, John Dominis//Time Life Pictures, Stephen Dunn, Focus on Sport, Bob Gomel/Time & Life Pictures, Otto Greule Jr/Stringer, Scott Halleran/Allsport, Will Hart, Ralph Morse//Time Life Pictures, National Baseball Hall of Fame Library/MLB Photos, Olen Collection/Diamond Images, Hy Peskin//Time Life Pictures, Photo File, Photo File/MLB Photos, Louis Requena/MLB Photos, Robert Riger, George Silk//Time Life Pictures, Jamie Squire, William Vandivert/Time Life Pictures)

Library of Congress Cataloging-in-Publication Data

Nichols, John, 1966-
The story of the Los Angeles Dodgers / by John Nichols.
p. cm. — (Baseball: the great American game)
Includes index.
ISBN-13: 978-1-58341-491-0
1. Los Angeles Dodgers (Baseball team)—History—Juvenile literature. I. Title. II. Series.

GV875.L6 N53 2007
796.3570979494—dc22   2006028074

First Edition
9 8 7 6 5 4 3 2 1

Cover: Outfielder Duke Snider
Page 1: Pitcher Sandy Koufax
Page 3: Pitcher Eric Gagne

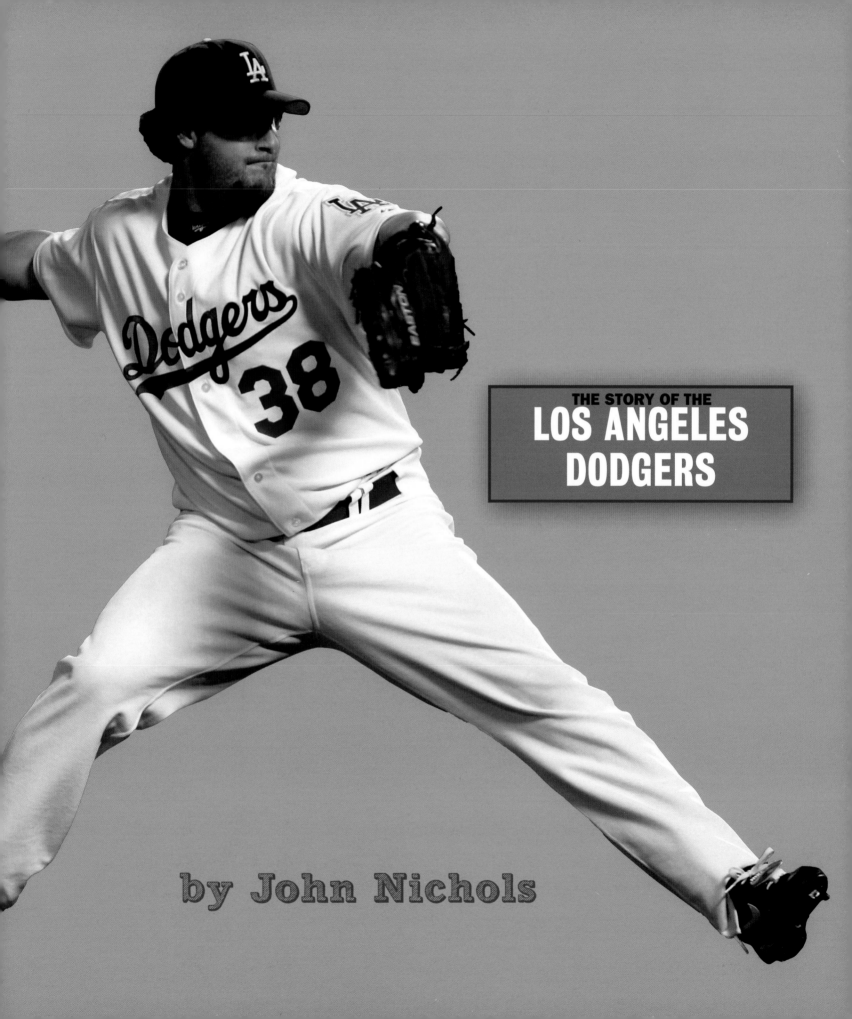

THE STORY OF THE
LOS ANGELES DODGERS

by John Nichols

1988 DODGERS

Los Angeles Dodgers

The Los Angeles Dodgers are facing the heavily favored Oakland A's in the 1988 World Series, and they are about to lose Game 1 in front of 50,000 hushed L.A. fans. Trailing 4–3 in the ninth inning, with two outs and a runner on first, the Dodgers make a desperate move, sending injured star outfielder Kirk Gibson to the plate as a pinch hitter. Barely able to walk, Gibson battles Oakland's ace reliever, Dennis Eckersley, to a full count. Then, down to his last strike, the injured slugger belts the next pitch over the right-field fence, giving the Dodgers a miraculous 5–4 victory. As Gibson hobbles around the bases pumping his right arm, Dodger Stadium shakes with the noise of the cheers. Inspired by Gibson's courageous feat, the Dodgers will go on to defeat the mighty A's and capture the franchise's sixth World Series title. It is a moment that summarizes the Dodgers' spirit. Never give up. Never give in.

EARLY SUCCESS IN BROOKLYN

L os Angeles, California, is a place to see stars. Home to Hollywood and many television studios, Los Angeles is widely regarded as the entertainment capital of the world. The city is famous for its movie-star citizens, glamorous stores, and sun-splashed weather. Tourists come from all over the world to visit the "City of Angels."

While the people of Los Angeles love their movie idols, they also have a deep passion for sports. The city is home to professional teams in hockey, basketball, and soccer, but Los Angeles's most beloved franchise was also its first: the Los Angeles Dodgers of Major League Baseball. The Dodgers are one of the oldest teams in the game, dating back to 1890, when they joined the National League (NL) as a team in Brooklyn, New York. Back then, fans walking to the ballpark had to dart across Brooklyn's busy trolley tracks, dodging the streetcars. That led local writers to dub the team the "Trolley Dodgers," a name that was eventually shortened to Dodgers.

In the early years of the franchise, the Brooklyn team was known by a number of names, including the Bridegrooms and Superbas; Dodgers would not find permanent status as the team's name until the early 1930s. In their

EBBETS FIELD

Ebbets Field, home to the Brooklyn Dodgers from 1913 until 1957, was well-known for its charm. Built when automobiles were owned only by the wealthy, the stadium featured fewer than 500 parking spaces. Instead, fans flocked to the ballpark using New York's streetcars, subways, and buses. Upon arrival, fans were greeted by the stadium's brick archways, a classic feature often imitated in modern stadiums. After buying a ticket, fans entered a marble rotunda that featured a 27-foot-high ceiling, from which a chandelier made of crystal baseball bats and balls hung. On the field, the stadium featured peculiar dimensions and an outfield fence that offered a variety of angles and heights. A ball hit down the right-field line had to travel a mere 297 feet to be a home run, while a 402-foot blast to right-center-field would fall just short of the fence. Many Brooklyn fans grew up and grew old attending games at Ebbets Field. For them, the stadium represented a simple, happy time. When Ebbets Field was leveled in 1960, people wept in the streets. Dodgers outfielder Duke Snider summed up the fans' emotions best when he said, "When they tore down Ebbets Field, they tore down a little piece of me."

DODGERS

[7]

PITCHER · SANDY KOUFAX

Arguably the most dominant pitcher in the history of major-league baseball, Sandy Koufax had a career that was like a comet streaking across the night sky—dazzlingly brilliant and then gone all too quickly. After battling control problems early in his career, Koufax posted an astounding 129 victories between 1961 and 1966. Blessed with an overpowering fastball and a knee-buckling curve, the left-hander hurled four no-hitters in the space of four seasons. Forced to retire at age 31 due to an arthritic elbow, Koufax became, at age 36, the youngest man ever inducted into the Baseball Hall of Fame.

STATS

Dodgers seasons: 1955–66

Height: 6-2

Weight: 210

- **4-time NL leader in strikeouts**
- **3-time Cy Young Award winner**
- **165 career wins**
- **2.76 career ERA**

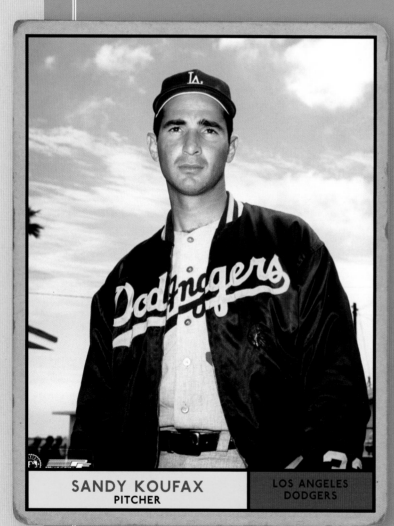

SANDY KOUFAX
PITCHER

LOS ANGELES
DODGERS

Joe McGinnity made his big-league debut at 28 years old and was still pitching in the minor leagues at 54.

JOE McGINNITY

first season in the NL, the Brooklyn Bridegrooms won the pennant, and the club went on to capture two more league championships in 1899 and 1900. Two stars of those early years were pitcher "Iron Man" Joe McGinnity and outfielder "Wee Willie" Keeler. McGinnity earned his nickname for his tireless arm and was known to often pitch both games of a double-header. The 5-foot-4 Keeler, meanwhile, hit for a high average by following a simple strategy of "hit 'em where they ain't."

"WEE WILLIE" KEELER – The always cheerful outfielder played like a giant in 1897, batting .432, getting 243 hits, and stringing together a 44-game hitting streak—an NL record that still stands. Among those hits were some of his famously masterful bunts.

CATCHER · ROY CAMPANELLA

"Campy," as Roy Campanella was called, was a standout in every phase of the game. Quick and agile behind the plate, he possessed such a cannon of an arm that opposing base runners rarely challenged him. At the plate, the burly catcher hit for power and was outstanding in clutch situations. Along with his rare skill, Campanella played with great joy and enthusiasm, and his friendly, easygoing personality made him a fan favorite. Campanella's career was cut tragically short when he was paralyzed in a car accident after the 1957 season. The Dodgers retired his number 39 uniform in 1972.

STATS

Dodgers seasons: 1948–57

Height: 5-8

Weight: 200

• 3-time NL MVP

• 242 career HR

• 8-time All-Star

• 1953 NL leader in RBI (142)

ROY CAMPANELLA
CATCHER

LOS ANGELES
DODGERS

FIRST BASEMAN · GIL HODGES

One of the best first basemen of his era, Hodges was a deft fielder and a powerful hitter. A rare right-handed first baseman, Hodges was known for his sure glove and ability to prevent errors by scooping up even the poorest throws from his fellow infielders. At the plate, he was especially dangerous with men on base, driving in 100 or more runs in 7 straight seasons. Regarded as one of the game's true gentlemen, Hodges was a fan favorite. When he slumped at the start of the 1953 season, a New York priest famously told his congregation, "Keep the 10 Commandments and pray for Gil Hodges."

GIL HODGES
FIRST BASEMAN

LOS ANGELES
DODGERS

STATS

Dodgers seasons: 1943, 1947–61

Height: 6-2

Weight: 200

- **370 career HR**

- **14 career grand slams**

- **3-time Gold Glove winner**

- **8-time All-Star**

In 1901, a new league was formed called the American League (AL). In 1903, the two rival leagues decided that their respective champions should meet in a postseason series that would decide which team and league was best. Today, the World Series, as it came to be known, is still the crowning glory of the big-league baseball season.

Unfortunately for Brooklyn fans, it would be a number of years before their team would get its first crack at a World Series championship. In fact, it wasn't until 1916 that Brooklyn—then led by popular manager Wilbert "Uncle Robbie" Robinson—finally won the NL pennant again. In the World Series, however, Robinson's club fell to the Boston Red Sox, four games to one.

Brooklyn returned to the World Series stage again in 1920. Led by hard-hitting outfielder Zack Wheat and pitcher Clarence "Dazzy" Vance, the Dodgers hoped to finally win a title for their beloved manager. Unfortunately, Brooklyn came up short again, this time losing the championship to the Cleveland Indians.

Robinson's reign as manager lasted from 1914 to 1931. His popularity was so great in New York that, during much of his tenure, the team was actually known as the "Robins." After the 1920 World Series, Brooklyn would not contend again for some time, but Robinson's ability to coax great play out of average players cemented his highly regarded legacy. "Robbie made a lot of good teams out of bad teams," noted Chicago Cubs manager Joe McCarthy.

BREAKING BARRIERS WITH JACKIE ROBINSON

The Dodgers teams of the 1930s were not very good. Known to their fans as the "Daffy Dodgers," many of the team's players were more famous for their glaring faults than their talents. A prime example was outfielder Babe Herman, who was excellent at the plate but a mistake waiting to happen in the field. "Every fly ball was an adventure for Babe," said Dodgers catcher Al Lopez. Despite the Dodgers' bumbling ways, Brooklyn fans took the players to their hearts, lovingly referring to the team as "Dem Bums."

Toward the end of the '30s, the Dodgers began to improve under the guidance of fiery manager Leo Durocher, who instilled discipline in the previously daffy Dodgers. By 1941, Brooklyn had assembled a roster featuring such stalwarts as shortstop Harold "Pee Wee" Reese and first baseman Dolph Camilli. The rejuvenated Dodgers stormed to the 1941 NL pennant and met the mighty New York Yankees in the World Series. The Dodgers lost to their crosstown rivals in five games, the first of what would be many championship clashes to come between the two teams.

Brooklyn stars Dolph Camilli (left) and Pee Wee Reese (second from right) with Dodgers teammates in 1942.

As the 1940s wore on, Dodgers president and general manager Branch Rickey became convinced that the time was right to break baseball's long-standing, unwritten rule that banned African American players from the major leagues. Under Rickey's direction, the Dodgers heavily scouted the Negro Leagues, where black players were allowed to play, looking for a man with the right talent and character to carry the burden of being the first black player in the majors.

In 1947, Rickey found his man. Just days before the season opener, the Dodgers signed second baseman Jackie Robinson. A tremendous athlete and a fierce competitor, Robinson was a fine player, but what caught Rickey's eye was Robinson's inner strength. When confronted with racism, Rickey wanted a player "with enough guts *not* to fight back."

Robinson faced hostility and jeers from many opponents and fans during his time with the Dodgers in the late 1940s and '50s, but he answered every taunt with his bat, his glove, and his base running. In his first season, Robinson hit .297, stole 29 bases, and scored 125 runs in leading the Dodgers to another NL pennant. For his efforts, Robinson earned the first-ever NL Rookie of the Year award. Robinson went on to play 10 stellar seasons with the Dodgers and eventually became the first African American to enter the Baseball Hall of Fame. "They said the most hateful things in the world to Jackie," said Dodgers outfielder Carl Furillo, "and it bothered him something fierce, but

BRANCH RICKEY: BASEBALL VISIONARY

Branch Rickey was a man who had vision. Perhaps most famous as the general manager who signed Jackie Robinson to the Dodgers and ended baseball's longtime exclusion of African American players, Rickey also contributed many other ideas and innovations that live on in the game today. Rickey is widely credited for inventing the minor-league farm system that trains and feeds talent to major-league clubs. He also was responsible for creating the first full-time spring-training facility, in Vero Beach, Florida; called "Dodgertown," the sprawling practice facility has been the training ground for Dodgers stars since 1948. Rickey is also credited with being the first to encourage the use of now-commonplace baseball equipment such as batting cages, pitching machines, and batting helmets. During his reign as president and general manager of the Dodgers (1942–50), Rickey used his great organizational skills and keen eye for talent to build the team that would become the "Boys of Summer"—the core of stars that would bring Brooklyn its first and only World Series title. Always thinking one step ahead of his peers, Rickey was famous for saying, "Luck is the residue of design."

they only hurt themselves, as it just made Jackie play that much harder."

In 1949, the Dodgers won their third NL pennant of the decade, but unfortunately, they also suffered their third World Series defeat, each time at the hands of the Yankees. Long-suffering Brooklyn fans longed for the day when their beloved "Bums" would finally beat the "Bronx Bombers," and "Wait until next year!" became the unofficial rallying cry of the Dodgers faithful.

JACKIE ROBINSON

JACKIE ROBINSON – There was never a dull moment when Robinson was on the base paths. The swift second baseman took a daredevil approach to base running, sometimes getting caught in between-bases rundowns and still managing to advance.

A SIMPLE ACT OF BROTHERHOOD

On April 15, 1947, Jackie Robinson became the first African American to play in the major leagues. Robinson's accomplishment is widely celebrated today as a great moment in history, but at the time, his joining the Dodgers caused a storm of controversy. In nearly every ballpark, Robinson was taunted and jeered mercilessly by bigoted opposing fans and players. He received numerous death threats, and several teams threatened to boycott games in which he played. During one of Robinson's first road games, the Dodgers were playing against the Cincinnati Reds. The Reds players and crowd taunted Robinson relentlessly, whether he was in the field or at the plate. Eventually the crowd also began to harrass Dodgers shortstop Pee Wee Reese. Reese, the Dodgers' captain, was a Southerner who hailed from the state of Kentucky, and the hecklers tore into him for playing with a black man. In answer to the taunts, Reese walked across the infield during a break in the game and put his arm around Robinson's shoulders. "He didn't say a word, but he looked over at the chaps who were yelling at me and just stared," said Robinson. "He kept staring, and after a bit, the taunts stopped. . . . I will never forget what he did."

SECOND BASEMAN · JACKIE ROBINSON

A terrific all-around athlete, Jackie Robinson was the first person to letter in four sports in the same year at the University of California at Los Angeles. Robinson played baseball with reckless abandon. With his great speed and daring, he became the spark plug for the Dodgers' offense; during his career, Robinson stole home an incredible 19 times. As the first African American player in the major leagues, Robinson had to be better than good. He had to be great—and courageous. In honor of his contributions to the game, Robinson's number 42 uniform was retired by all major-league teams in 1997.

STATS

Dodgers seasons: 1947–56

Height: 5-11

Weight: 204

- .311 career BA
- 1947 NL Rookie of the Year
- 1949 NL MVP
- 6-time All-Star

JACKIE ROBINSON
SECOND BASEMAN

LOS ANGELES
DODGERS

JOHNNY PODRES

THE "BOYS OF SUMMER"

By the 1950s, Brooklyn had built a deep and powerful line-up. Captained by Pee Wee Reese, the Dodgers boasted a roster bristling with stars such as Robinson, catcher Roy Campanella, center fielder Edwin "Duke" Snider, first base-man Gil Hodges, and pitchers Don Newcombe and Carl Erskine. Together, they dominated the NL throughout the decade and became folk heroes to adoring Brooklyn fans. Because they played and won together for so many years, Dodgers fans lovingly referred to the group of stars as the "Boys of Summer."

The Dodgers won NL pennants in 1952 and 1953, but, as had happened in 1941, 1947, and 1949, the team was then beaten in the World Series by the Yankees. Finally, in 1955, the wait for "next year" ended. Sparked by Snider's 42 home runs and Newcombe's 20 pitching victories, the Dodgers roared to the NL pennant under manager Walter Alston. In the World Series, the Dodgers again faced their nemesis, the Yankees, but this time they came out on top, as 23-year-old pitcher Johnny Podres threw a complete-game, 2–0 shutout in Game 7 to deliver a championship to Brooklyn. "It's like I died and

Gil Hodges played one game in 1943, spent four years in the Marines, then returned for 15 more Dodgers seasons.

SHORTSTOP · MAURY WILLS

As a young minor-leaguer, Maury Wills was thought to be too small and scrawny, and scouts doubted that he had the makings of a major-leaguer. After years of hard work, though, Wills finally did get called up by the Dodgers at age 26. Although Wills's career got off to a slow start, everything he did thereafter was fast. The speedy shortstop established himself as one of the premier leadoff hitters and base stealers in the game's history. In 1962, he stole 104 bases, setting a major-league record that would stand for 12 years. Wills was a key contributor in the Dodgers' World Series triumphs in 1963 and 1965.

STATS

Dodgers seasons: 1959–66, 1969–72

Height: 5-11

Weight: 170

- **1962 NL MVP**
- **6-time NL leader in stolen bases**
- **2-time Gold Glove winner**
- **586 career stolen bases**

MAURY WILLS
SHORTSTOP

LOS ANGELES
DODGERS

went to heaven," said Dodgers third baseman Jim "Junior" Gilliam. "I'm so happy we could finally do this for our fans."

The Dodgers won the NL pennant again the next season and again met the Yankees in the World Series, but this time the outcome was less heavenly in Brooklyn. The Yankees took the series in seven games.

After the 1957 season, Dodgers team president Walter O'Malley decided to move the franchise to Los Angeles. Brooklyn's home ballpark, Ebbets Field, was aging and seated only 32,000 fans. O'Malley had lobbied the city of New York for a new ballpark for years, but to no avail. When Los Angeles offered to build the Dodgers a beautiful new, 56,000-seat stadium, O'Malley made the difficult decision to move the team west. "I know this will be unpopular with our loyal Brooklyn fans," said O'Malley, "but I have to do what is right for the team."

KOUFAX AND "DOUBLE D"

The Dodgers' home during their first few years in California was the Los Angeles Coliseum, a converted football stadium. But by 1962, the team had moved into the ballpark it still calls home today, Dodger Stadium.

Before the team settled into its new ballpark, the last of the Boys of Summer had one final hurrah to share with their new West Coast fans. Led by Snider and Hodges, the Dodgers captured the 1959 NL pennant with an 88–68 record. In the World Series, Los Angeles rode pitcher Larry Sherry's two victories to defeat the Chicago White Sox in six games. "I think our win in 1959 cemented the bond between the Los Angeles fans and the team," said Alston. "That championship finally made us their team."

By 1963, the face of the team had changed. Nearly all of the old Brooklyn heroes were gone, and the Dodgers had rebuilt around strong pitching, defense, and speed. In the starting rotation, the team featured two of the game's biggest stars in left-hander Sandy Koufax and right-hander Don "Double D" Drysdale. Koufax possessed a blazing fastball and perhaps the best curveball the game has ever seen. The hulking, 6-foot-6 Drysdale also threw hard but was best known for his fiercely competitive personality. "Don was a guy who owned

DODGERS

DON DRYSDALE

DON DRYSDALE – Batting against Drysdale could be a scary—and sometimes painful—experience, as the intimidating pitcher liked to keep hitters nervous, plunking 154 batsmen in his career. He spent all of his 14 big-league seasons with the Dodgers.

A GIANT RIVALRY

Up until the late 1950s, New York City was home to three major-league teams. The Yankees played in the AL, while the Dodgers and New York Giants competed in the NL. Before interleague play began in 1997, teams from opposite leagues did not play one another unless they met in the World Series. So while the Dodgers did strike up a rivalry with the Yankees due to their many meetings in the World Series, it was the Giants who proved to be Brooklyn's "everyday and every year" rival. Season after season, Brooklyn's blue-collar fans would cheer for their "Bums" to defeat the Giants, whose home park, the Polo Grounds, was located in the more affluent borough of Manhattan. Since 1890, the two teams have combined to win 39 NL pennants and 11 World Series. "For a while, it seemed like if it wasn't us, it was them," said Dodgers skipper Leo Durocher, who eventually managed both teams. After the 1957 season, both teams left for new cities on the West Coast—the Giants in San Francisco and the Dodgers in Los Angeles—but the rivalry continues. "It's the first thing they teach you," said Dodgers pitcher Eric Gagne. "You gotta beat the Giants."

THIRD BASEMAN · RON CEY

Nicknamed "The Penguin" on account of his short, stocky build and choppy running stride, Cey manned the "hot corner" in Los Angeles for 12 seasons. Despite his modest stature, Cey generated considerable power, hitting 20 or more home runs in 6 straight seasons. In the 1981 World Series, Cey was beaned by hard-throwing Yankees pitcher Rich Gossage. Showing grit and determination, Cey returned to the lineup and went on to hit .350 for the series, leading the Dodgers to victory. For his efforts, Cey was named co-MVP of the series along with teammates Pedro Guerrero (outfielder) and Steve Yeager (catcher).

RON CEY
THIRD BASEMAN

LOS ANGELES
DODGERS

STATS

Dodgers seasons: 1971–82

Height: 5-10

Weight: 185

- **316 career HR**
- **1,139 career RBI**
- **6-time All-Star**
- **1,868 career hits**

WILLIE DAVIS

the plate," said Dodgers catcher Johnny Roseboro, "and if a hitter looked too comfy up there, Double D would put him on the seat of his pants."

Koufax and Drysdale gave the Dodgers an awesome one-two pitching punch, while the offense was led by speedy second baseman Maury Wills and hard-hitting outfielders Tommy Davis and Willie Davis. The Los Angeles teams of the 1960s did not try to overpower opponents with home runs. Instead, they used their great team speed to manufacture runs on the base paths and played great defense behind stellar pitching.

LEFT FIELDER · ZACK WHEAT

Described by one reporter as "165 pounds of scrap iron, rawhide, and guts," Zack Wheat played in more games than any other player in Dodgers history. A sweet-swinging, left-handed batter, Wheat was an extraordinarily good curveball hitter—so good, in fact, that New York Giants manager John McGraw forbade his pitchers from throwing him any.

Remarkably consistent, Wheat's batting average topped .300 in 13 of his 19 seasons. He was a quiet leader who was widely respected for playing the game hard but clean. In his nearly two-decade career, Wheat was never ejected from a ballgame.

ZACK WHEAT
LEFT FIELDER

LOS ANGELES DODGERS

STATS

Dodgers seasons: 1909–26

Height: 5-10

Weight: 165

- **2,884 career hits**

- **.317 career BA**

- **1918 NL leader in BA (.335)**

- **1,289 career runs scored**

In 1963, this Los Angeles crew captured another NL pennant. In the World Series, the Dodgers once again faced their old rivals, the Yankees. This time, the Dodgers swept New York in four straight games. Los Angeles's pitching throttled the normally powerful Yankees, allowing only four runs the entire series.

In 1965, Koufax and Drysdale teamed up to win 49 games, propelling the Dodgers to another NL pennant. In the World Series, Los Angeles faced the Minnesota Twins, who were led by slugging third baseman Harmon Killebrew. After losing the first two contests, the Dodgers stormed back to even the series at three games apiece. In Game 7, Koufax's three-hit, complete-game shutout delivered a 2–0 win and the title for Los Angeles. "He pitched a shutout in Game 7 three days after he pitched a shutout in Game 5," said Dodgers second baseman Jim Lefebvre. "Sometimes I wonder if Sandy is human."

Koufax and the Dodgers advanced to the World Series again in 1966, but this time they proved to be human, losing to the Baltimore Orioles in four straight games. After the series, Koufax retired. Still in his prime but in constant pain due to an arthritic elbow, one of the game's all-time greats left the stage at age 31.

LASORDA TAKES THE REINS

T he Dodgers remained a formidable team through the end of the 1960s and into the '70s. The one constant through those years was the leadership of manager Walter Alston. A quiet teacher of the game, Alston guided the Dodgers to a total of four world championships and seven NL pennants. Toward the end of the 1976 season, Alston finally retired and was replaced by the team's third base coach, Tommy Lasorda. The talkative and emotional Lasorda was nearly the exact opposite of Alston, but he achieved the same results, as the Dodgers remained an NL power.

By the mid-1970s, though, the Dodgers had become a different kind of team. They still featured great pitching with the likes of Don Sutton, but the team's offense had morphed into a power-hitting machine. In 1977, first baseman Steve Garvey, third baseman Ron Cey, and outfielders Dusty Baker and Reggie Smith all hit 30 or more home runs, making the Dodgers the first team in baseball history to have four players accomplish the feat in the same season.

The Dodgers reached the World Series in 1977 and 1978, but both times they were defeated by their old pinstriped foes, the Yankees. In 1981, Los Angeles again reached the World Series and faced the Yankees, but this time it had an

Under popular manager Tommy Lasorda's 22-year reign, the Dodgers suffered only 6 losing seasons.

STEVE GARVEY

STEVE GARVEY – Garvey was one of baseball's top iron men, playing in a league-record 1,207 consecutive games from 1975 to 1983. He found the national spotlight in 1974 by capturing the NL MVP award and went on to play in 10 All-Star Games.

CENTER FIELDER · DUKE SNIDER

Snider was the centerpiece of the great Brooklyn teams of the 1950s. A swift, sure-handed fielder, he ranged over the outfield like a gazelle. At the plate, Snider batted third in the Dodgers' potent lineup and earned fame with his mammoth home runs. A clutch postseason performer, Snider hit four home runs in two different World Series and clobbered 11 total World Series home runs in his career. Nicknamed the "Duke of Flatbush" (Flatbush was a well-to-do Brooklyn neighborhood) by fans, Snider was baseball royalty in New York City. Fittingly, he belted the last home run ever hit at Ebbets Field.

DUKE SNIDER
CENTER FIELDER

LOS ANGELES
DODGERS

STATS

Dodgers seasons: 1947–62

Height: 6-0

Weight: 190

- **407 career HR**

- **1,333 career RBI**

- **8-time All-Star**

- **Baseball Hall of Fame inductee (1980)**

FERNANDO VALENZUELA

The youngest of 12 children in a Mexican farm family, Fernando Valenzuela became an unlikely hero.

edge. Twenty-year-old rookie pitcher Fernando Valenzuela had burst onto the scene that year, capturing the hearts of Dodgers fans with his dazzling screwball and uncanny ability to win big games.

By the time the Dodgers reached the World Series, Los Angeles was completely immersed in "Fernandomania," a term coined to describe the hysteria surrounding the team's young star. The Dodgers dropped the first two games to the Yankees but came back to win Game 3 behind a gritty performance from Valenzuela. The inspired Dodgers then won the next three games and the series. "We had them on the ropes, but that kid [Valenzuela] turned the series around," said Yankees outfielder Dave Winfield.

After several disappointing seasons, the Dodgers went on a surprising run in 1988. Led by another star pitcher, right-hander Orel Hershiser, and outfielder Kirk Gibson, the Dodgers won the NL Western Division (the league was split into two divisions in 1969) with a 94–67 record and beat the heavily favored New York Mets in the NL Championship Series (NLCS).

In the World Series, the underdog Dodgers used a miraculous, game-winning home run from an injured Gibson in Game 1 and two masterful performances from Hershiser in Games 2 and 5 to defeat the heavily favored Oakland A's. "Nobody gave us a chance to beat the Mets, and when we beat them, everybody thought we'd get steamrolled by the A's," said Dodgers outfielder Mike Marshall. "We took it personally, and I guess we showed them."

The Dodgers continued to contend through the early 1990s. Led by stars such as slugging catcher Mike Piazza and pitcher Hideo Nomo, Los Angeles captured the NL West in 1995 and the NL Wild Card in 1996 (Wild Card teams were added to baseball's postseason in 1995). At the end of the 1996 season, Lasorda retired. For his long and successful service, he was inducted into the Baseball Hall of Fame in 1997.

 OREL HERSHISER

THE "BULLDOG" BESTS "DOUBLE D"

In 1968, Dodgers pitcher Don Drysdale set a record that many people thought would last forever. The big hurler fans liked to call "Double D" threw six consecutive shutouts on his way to logging a major-league-record 58.2 straight scoreless innings. "Unbelievable," said Dodgers first baseman Wes Parker. "He's just flat unhittable." The record stood until 1988, when a slender Dodgers pitcher by the name of Orel Hershiser blanked the opposition for 59 straight innings. Hershiser broke the record during his last start of the regular season, whitewashing the San Diego Padres for 10 innings. Unlike Drysdale, Hershiser was slight and almost scholarly looking, but he shared Drysdale's fierce, competitive spirit. Early in his career, Dodgers manager Tommy Lasorda gave Hershiser the nickname "Bulldog" because of his tenacity on the mound. In the 1988 postseason, Hershiser went on to throw eight more scoreless innings before finally allowing a run. His regular-season scoreless streak ended the next year on opening day, when he surrendered a run against the Cincinnati Reds in the first inning. "Bulldog's record is even more amazing because he isn't the biggest or the strongest," said Lasorda. "But he's strongest where it counts—in his heart."

UP-AND-DOWN DODGERS

T he 1990s were a mix of highs and lows for the Dodgers. On the upside, the franchise was still turning out top-notch talent. Between 1992 and 1996, the team became the first ever to produce five consecutive Rookie of the Year award winners—a string of young stars that included first baseman Eric Karros, Piazza, outfielder Raul Mondesi, Nomo, and outfielder Todd Hollandsworth. On the downside, the '90s was the first decade since the '30s that the club did not make at least one World Series appearance. The 1998 season marked the end of an era, as the O'Malley family—owners of the team for five decades—sold the club to the Fox Entertainment Group.

With new ownership, the Dodgers hoped to find better luck with some new tactics. For most of its history, the team had built from within, rarely making big trades or signing expensive free agents. The Dodgers had always seemed able to harvest new talent from their highly productive minor-league system. But after a number of down seasons, the Dodgers decided to tinker with their time-honored philosophy and rebuild their roster from the outside. From 2000 to 2003, stars such as pitcher Kevin Brown and outfielders Gary Sheffield and Shawn Green were brought in from other teams

RIGHT FIELDER · CARL FURILLO

Known as "The Reading Rifle" on account of his Pennsylvania hometown and his powerful throws, Furillo was a fixture in right field for the Dodgers for 15 seasons. After he led the league in outfield assists in both 1950 and 1951, opposing base runners rarely challenged his strong right arm. Furillo was a very slow runner, but he compensated by carefully studying where opposing players typically hit the ball and using the information to position himself correctly in the field. A consistent and powerful hitter, Furillo batted .300 or better 5 times during his career and drove in 90 or more runs in 6 seasons.

CARL FURILLO
RIGHT FIELDER

LOS ANGELES
DODGERS

STATS

Dodgers seasons: 1946–60

Height: 6-0

Weight: 190

- **1953 NL leader in BA (.344)**

- **.299 career BA**

- **2-time All-Star**

- **1,058 career RBI**

BRAD PENNY

Big hurler Brad Penny put together his finest season in 2006, going 16–9 while striking out 148 batters.

THE DODGER DOG

One of Dodger Stadium's biggest attractions has never thrown a pitch or stolen a base, but it has been a big hit with the fans since 1962. *It* is the Dodger Dog. The 10-inch, all-pork hot dog, wrapped in a steamed bun, is the top-selling hot dog in baseball. Each season, 26 million hot dogs are consumed in major-league stadiums around the country, but in Los Angeles, the Dodger Dog is king. Dodgers fans consume more that 1.6 million of the ballpark delicacies—nearly 100,000 more than the next-biggest hot dog-loving park (Coors Field, home of the Colorado Rockies). The Dodger Dog first came on the scene during the team's inaugural season in Dodger Stadium. The team's concessions director, Thomas Arthur, wanted to offer fans something bigger and better than the normal ballpark hot dog. Arthur modeled the Dodger Dog after the foot-long hot dogs he ate as a child in New York City. "The Dodger Dog is very much a part of the baseball experience in Los Angeles," said longtime Dodgers radio broadcaster Vin Scully. "It's hard to imagine enjoying a game without one." Nearly 50 years after its introduction to California fans, the Dodger Dog still reigns supreme in Los Angeles.

to help put the Dodgers back in contention. During those years, however, Los Angeles could do no better than second place in its division. "We kept looking for the quick fix, and there is no such thing," said catcher Paul Lo Duca. "We weren't doing things the Dodger way."

In 2004, the Dodgers returned to the playoffs behind tremendous seasons from two homegrown players. Third baseman Adrian Beltre slammed 48 home runs, and pitcher Eric Gagne earned 45 saves to propel the team to the top of the NL West. The Dodgers lost to the St. Louis Cardinals in the NL Division Series (NLDS), three games to one, but the postseason excitement raised hopes in L.A. once again.

After going just 71–91 in 2005, the Dodgers continued to add free-agent talent. In 2006, they put such players as speedy shortstop Rafael Furcal, slugging first baseman Nomar Garciaparra, and hurlers Brad Penny and Derek Lowe on the field. "We've got a solid mix of veterans and young guys," said Dodgers manager Grady Little. "We have a lot to prove, but I think this group can get it done."

The 2006 Dodgers streaked their way to an 88–74 record and the NL Wild Card berth in the playoffs, losing 13 of 14 games at one point during the season, then promptly winning 11 in a row. But Los Angeles could not keep up with the New York Mets in the NLDS, losing the series in three straight games.

The Los Angeles Dodgers are one of professional sports' most storied franchises. From its heyday in Brooklyn to its championships in Los Angeles, the team has provided its legions of fans with countless thrills. And while there have been heartbreaks, the Dodgers faithful have always had reason to believe that success was just around the corner. For no matter the odds, the Dodgers' theme is always the same: Never give up. Never give in.

NOMAR GARCIAPARRA – A California native, Garciaparra spent 10 seasons with the Boston Red Sox and Chicago Cubs before donning Dodgers blue. The shortstop played with an intensity that made him a fan favorite but also left him frequently injured.

MANAGER · WALTER ALSTON

When Walter Alston was a young minor-league player, he spent his off-seasons teaching grade school. There is no doubt Alston's ability to teach followed him over to his managing career. In his 23 seasons at the helm, the Dodgers won 7 NL pennants and 4 World Series. Quiet and studious, Alston taught generations of players the "Dodger way," a brand of baseball marked by good fundamentals, intelligence, and constant hustle. During an era when most managers sought job security by negotiating for multi-year contracts, the modest Alston managed for nearly a quarter of a century on a series of one-year agreements.

STATS

Dodgers seasons as manager: 1954–76

Height: 6-2

Weight: 195

Managerial Record: 2,040–1,613

World Series Championships: 1955, 1959, 1963, 1965

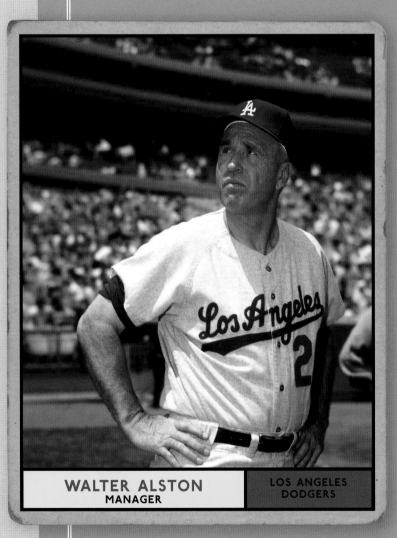

WALTER ALSTON
MANAGER

LOS ANGELES
DODGERS